Pam Wedgwood

Piano
Basics 1

A step-by-step piano method for the complete musician

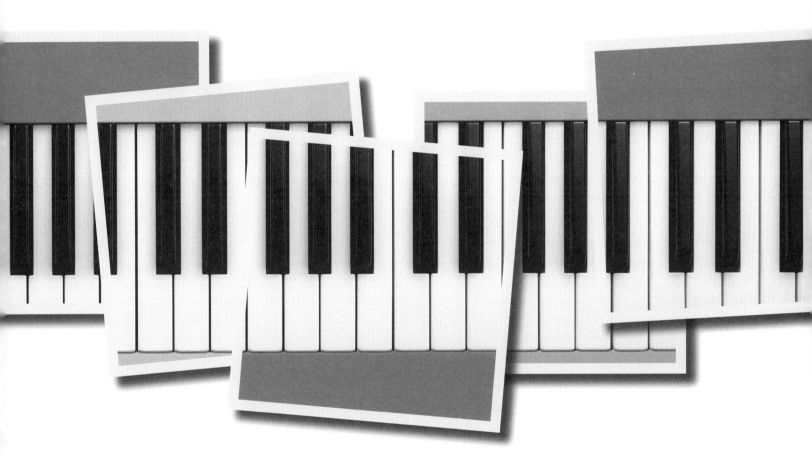

FABER *ff* MUSIC

Introduction

A note to pupils

Welcome to the world of music and to the piano – your journey is about to begin! In order to make lots of progress, try to play the piano every day, even if it is only for a short time. When you spot dice in the book they show that you are developing other musical skills as well as your piano playing – you can see what else is covered from the pictures below. Remember to entertain your family and friends by giving mini-concerts of the pieces as you learn them and show off what you can do! Most of all – have lots of fun!

A note to parents

Offering your child the opportunity to learn the piano is one of the most rewarding gifts you can give: the language of music is universal and can be enjoyed by everyone. Learning new skills can sometimes be a little daunting, but with your help and encouragement your child will acquire a wonderful skill for life. I hope this fun piano course will lead to a stimulating and exciting musical journey for all concerned.

A note to teachers

This piano course has been specifically written for children from around age 8 upwards, with the intention of developing musicianship skills alongside their piano playing. It progresses steadily, ensuring that your pupils have a thorough knowledge of all the notes and values covered by the end of the book. Many of the pieces have teacher's accompaniments to add to the enjoyment and stimulate progress. The dice which you will spot throughout the book highlight the different aspects of musicianship which are covered alongside the pieces:

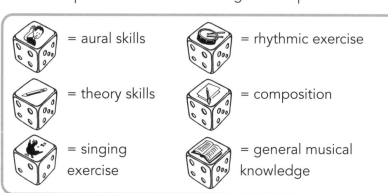

= aural skills

= rhythmic exercise

= theory skills

= composition

= singing exercise

= general musical knowledge

 For the online audio scan the QR code or go to: fabermusic.com/audio

 = the audio tracks have a two-bar count-in so pupils can play along.

All music by Pam Wedgwood unless otherwise stated.

To Jemima and Annabel

© 2013 by Faber Music Ltd
This edition first published in 2013
Bloomsbury House
74–77 Great Russell Street
London WC1B 3DA
Music processed by MacMusic
Cover designed by Chloë Alexander
Audio recorded and produced by Oliver Wedgwood
Printed in England by Caligraving Ltd
All rights reserved

ISBN10: 0-571-53762-6
EAN13: 978-0-571-53762-4

To buy Faber Music publications or to find out about the full range of titles available please contact your local music retailer or Faber Music sales enquiries:

Faber Music Ltd, Burnt Mill, Elizabeth Way, Harlow CM20 2HX
Tel: +44 (0) 1279 82 89 82   Fax: +44 (0) 1279 82 89 83
sales@fabermusic.com   fabermusicstore.com

Sitting at the piano

Checklist

- Sit on the front half of the seat and lean slightly forwards.
- When your hands are on the keys, your elbows and arms should be level with the keyboard.

Check your posture

- Sit tall but relax your shoulders.
- Your upper arms hang loosely from your shoulders.
- It's easy to sit with the wrong posture and slump. Always remember to sit up tall before you begin playing.

Your hand position

Stand up straight and let your hands hang down, completely relaxed and loose at your side. Your fingers will now be in the correct, softly-curved shape.

Place your hands over the piano keys and pretend you are holding a bubble: don't let it burst!

All fingers and thumbs!

In piano music your thumbs and fingers are indicated by numbers:

Top tip Draw around both of your hands on a piece of paper and number your thumbs and fingers.

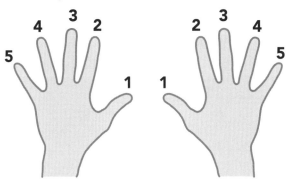

Remember your finger numbers

Place both hands on a flat surface then:
- tap your 1st fingers
- tap your 3rd fingers
- tap your 5th fingers
- tap your 2nd fingers
- tap your 4th fingers

Let's get playing

Finger tunes

Start on ANY white note and follow the finger numbers.

Play these patterns using your **right hand**:

> 1 This is up.   This is down.
> **1 2 3   3 2 1**
>
> Keep your fin – gers nice and round.
> **1   2   3   2   1   2   1**

> 2 Jump – ing jump – ing jump – ing Jack.
> **1   5   1   5   1   5   1**
>
> Fall – ing down   up – on his back!
> **5   4   3   2   1 1   1**

> 3 Three blind mice.   Three blind mice.
> **3   2   1   3   2   1**
>
> Had a crash   It was – n't nice!
> **1 2   3   4 3   2   1**

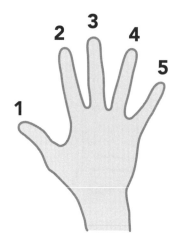

Keep thinking about your good hand position!

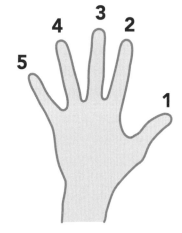

Practise your fingering on the piano lid or table top. Say each finger number as you tap it.

Play these patterns using your **left hand**:

> 1 Go - ing up and down a - gain
> **3   2 1 2   3   3   3**
>
> is like be - ing in an aer - o – plane.
> **3 2 2   3 1 2 1 1   1**

> 2 Ma – ry had a lit – tle cat
> **1   2 3 2 1 1 1**
>
> Who slept all day up-on the mat.
> **4   1 2 3 4 5 5   5**

> 3 Slid – ing down the wa – ter chute
> **1   2   3   4 5   3   1**
>
> Is such good fun it's just a hoot!
> **3 1   2   3   4 5 5   5**

Playing on the black keys

The black keys on the keyboard are arranged into groups of two and three.

Play all the black keys on your piano: can you spot the different groups?

Three pieces to make up

Make up your own black-key piece for each of these titles:

1 *Falling down a big black hole*

2 *Icicles*

3 *The traffic jam*

> If you find this tricky try playing with just one finger at first.

☐ Use fingers **2**, **3** and **4** of your left or right hand.

☐ You can play along with tracks 1, 2 or 3 or the teacher's accompaniments below.

☐ Think about how you can make your music match each title.

☐ You can play any black notes: go for it!

Falling down a big black hole accompaniment

Icicles accompaniment

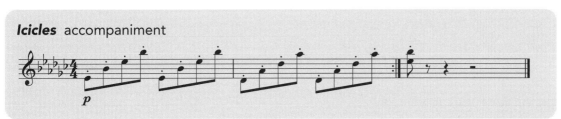

The traffic jam accompaniment

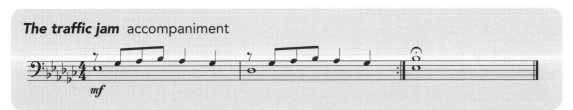

5

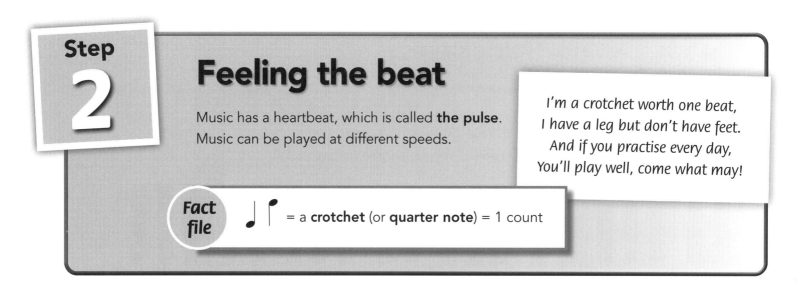

Step 2

Feeling the beat

Music has a heartbeat, which is called **the pulse**.
Music can be played at different speeds.

I'm a crotchet worth one beat,
I have a leg but don't have feet.
And if you practise every day,
You'll play well, come what may!

Fact file ♩ 𝅘𝅥 = a **crotchet** (or **quarter note**) = 1 count

---

(4) Get clapping

Clap a slow **pulse** in time with your teacher's accompaniment or the CD.

---

(5) Bouncing beat

(6) Try bouncing a ball to a regular beat (using tracks 4, 5 or 6, or any song you like). Using your strong hand, bounce the ball on one beat and catch it on the next. It takes a bit of practice! A tennis ball works well, but if you find that tricky, try a larger ball and use both hands.

Bounce the ball nearer the ground for a faster pulse.

---

(4) Time machine

Music is made up of notes of different lengths. We know how long notes last by looking at their shape and counting.

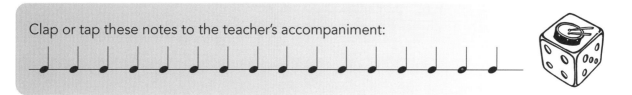

Clap or tap these notes to the teacher's accompaniment:

Get clapping / Time machine accompaniment

Two black-key pieces

 Fact file Notes are grouped into **bars** (or measures) by **barlines**. These pieces have four ♩ in each bar. At the end there is a **double barline**.

Use this group of black keys anywhere on the piano keyboard:

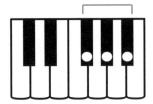

(7) Right on parade

Right hand: play ♩ beats and follow the finger numbers.

Use these fingers:

3 3 2 2 3 3 4 4 3 3 2 2 3 4 2 2

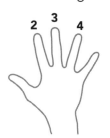

Are you playing a steady pulse, just as your heart beats?

(7) Left on parade

Left hand: follow the finger numbers and keep a steady pulse.

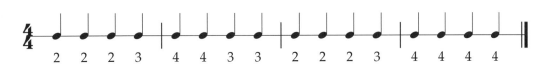

2 2 2 3 4 4 3 3 2 2 2 3 4 4 4 4

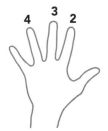

 Can you draw in four bars of crotchets (quarter notes) here? Don't forget the barlines!

$\frac{4}{4}$

Right / Left on parade accompaniment

Introducing ♩

I'm a minim, worth two beats,
I love to shop and buy some treats.
My head is empty, my leg is long,
Come and play a two-beat song.

8 Marching Martian minims

Tap, clap or drum this rhythm, then play it on these black keys.
Follow the fingering, with the right then left hand.

4/4 4 3 | 4 2 | 3 3 | 4 3 |

4 3 | 4 2 | 3 3 | 2 2 ‖

There are two ♩ in
each bar in this piece.
Can you spot the
barlines?

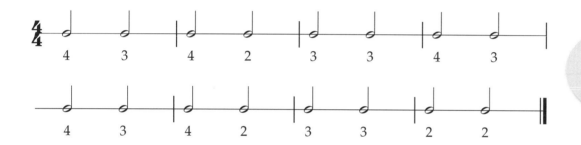

Draw in four bars of minims (half notes) here. Don't forget the barlines!

4/4

Keep practising! Aim to
play the piano every time
you walk past it.

Marching Martian minims accompaniment

All mixed up: ♩ and ♩

Using ♩ and ♩ notes together and both hands

Clever clogs

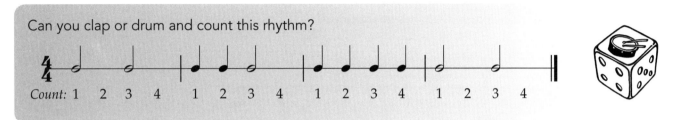

Can you clap or drum and count this rhythm?

Count: 1 2 3 4   1 2 3 4   1 2 3 4   1 2 3 4

Play the following pieces using this group of black notes in the right and left hands.
Remember to count the different note values! Each group is one bar.

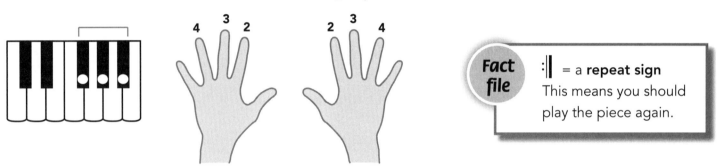

Fact file   :‖ = a **repeat sign**
This means you should play the piece again.

9 Chinese lanterns

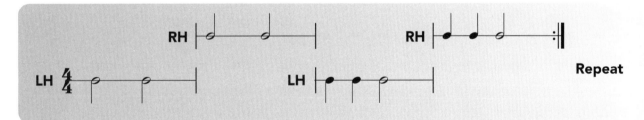

Repeat

9 Bouncing ball

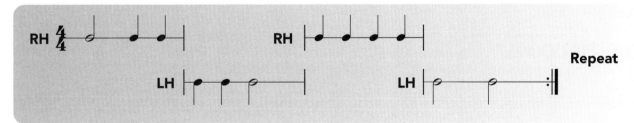

Repeat

Chinese lanterns / Bouncing ball accompaniment

Introducing o and 4/4

Fact file

o = a **semibreve** (or **whole note**) = 4 counts

4/4 at the start of the piece is a **time signature**.
It tells you there are four ♩ beats in each bar.

Semibreve four-beats is quite fat,
You'll need to count to move like that!
His head is full of empty space,
And he has no leg to keep in place!

Clap and count:

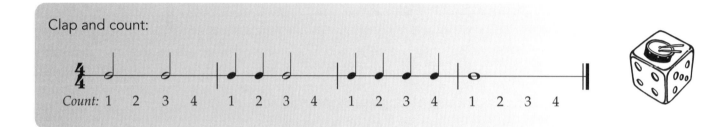

Count: 1 2 3 4   1 2 3 4   1 2 3 4   1 2 3 4

Play the following tunes using any black keys – with any finger!

(10) ## Dark chocolate sauce boogie with the right hand:

Can you see the repeat sign?

(10) ## Blackbird boogie with the left hand:

(10) ## Black-cat boogie with the right hand:

(10) ## Blackberry boogie with either hand:

All Boogies' accompaniments

Chief Inspector Rhythm

One note is missing from each bar – fill in the correct value.
Remember, a bar in $\frac{4}{4}$ always has four beats.

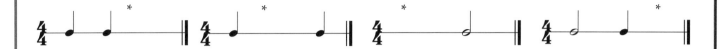

Two notes are missing from each of these bars:

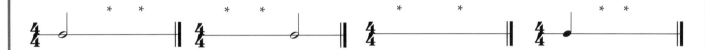

Play or clap one of these rhythms and ask your teacher to spot which one it is.

Make up your own one-bar rhythms using and **o**:

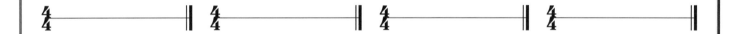

The stave

We read music from notes written on five lines. Together, these lines make a **stave**:

A **clef** at the start of any stave of music shows us whether the notes are high or low.

This is the **treble clef**, for higher (right-hand) notes:

This is the **bass clef**, for lower (left-hand) notes: ꝯ:

Draw around each clef then copy some of your own.

Step 3

Welcome to the white notes
Right-hand C, D, E

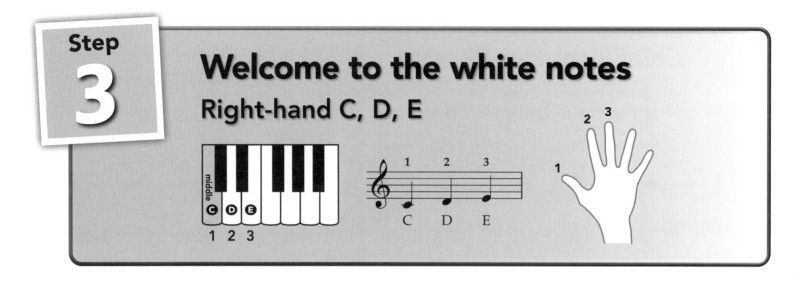

Say the note-names as you play:

Can you play all the Cs, Ds and Es on the piano?

11 White-note serenade

12 E-asy does it!

Can you sing back this melody?

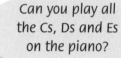

Your teacher will play C, D and E to you, then one note again – can you name which it is?

Fill in the note names: Fill in the notes: Write in your own notes:

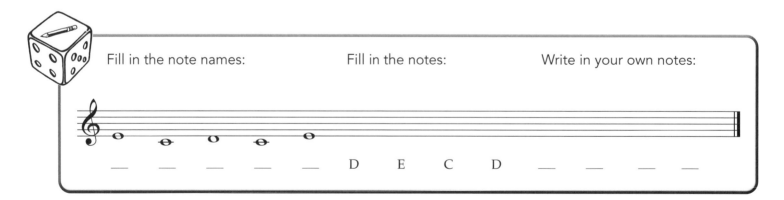

___   ___   ___   ___   ___   D   E   C   D   ___   ___   ___   ___

White-note serenade / E-asy does it accompaniments

Friends

My best friend is _____ He is in my class.
(She)

13 Chugging along

14 Ambulance sirens

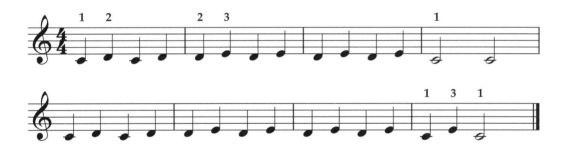

Can you clap the pulse of these pieces with the CD? Remember to keep a regular beat – like your heart or a clock ticking.

Draw a stave and treble clef on a large piece of paper. Add the notes C, D and E to it. Pin it up where you can look at it lots!

Compose your own tune using C, D and E.

Include 𝅝 𝅗𝅥 and ♩ Give it a title: _____

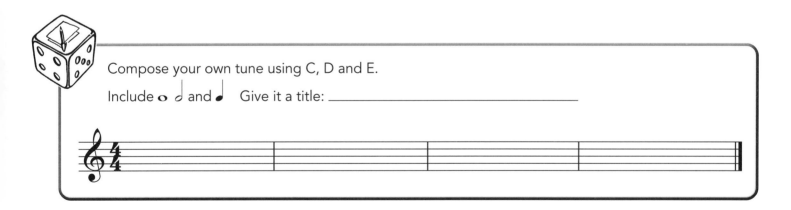

Chugging along / Ambulance sirens accompaniments

Left-hand A, B, C

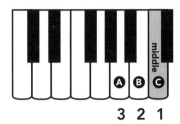  

Remember, the notes for the left hand are written in the **bass clef**.

Say the note-names as you play:

> *Can you play all the As, Bs and Cs on the piano?*

(15) Peek-a-boo

(16) Cheeky cherry

> Add these three notes to a bass clef and stave on the piece of paper you pinned up. Keep checking it!

Compose your own tune using A, B and C.

Include o ♩ and ♩ Give it a title: _____

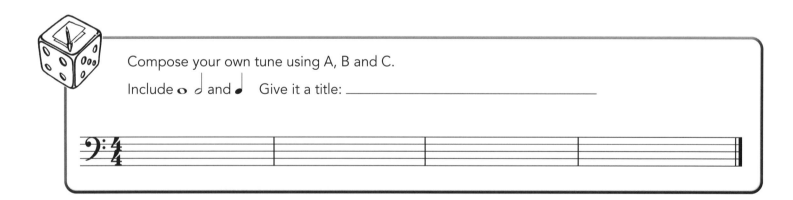

Peek-a-boo / Cheeky cherry accompaniments

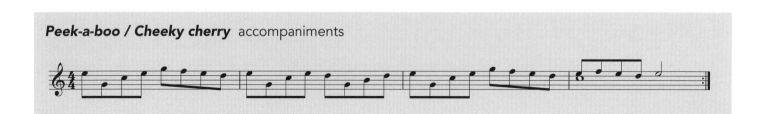

Picnic time!

Your teacher will play some phrases from these tunes – can you clap them back?

17 ## Swinging sausage rolls

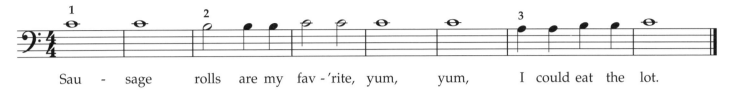

Sau - sage   rolls   are   my   fav - 'rite,   yum,   yum,   I   could   eat   the   lot.

18 ## Sandwich special

Cheese and   pic - kle,   eggs   and   ham.   But   my   fav - 'rite   one   is   JAM!

19 ## Strawberry heaven

Straw-ber-ries   and   cream,   straw-ber-ries   and   cream.   This   is   so   yum-my,   can   it   be   a   dream?

Sing these tunes as you play them.
Can you make up your own words for them?

Swinging sausage rolls accompaniment

Sandwich special accompaniment

Strawberry heaven accompaniment

Floating boxes

Join up the boxes to the correct clouds:

| A B C | C A B | E D C | C D E |

Write in the correct clef:

| B A C | D C E | A C B |

Join the musical notes to each of the letters, and fill in the missing clefs:

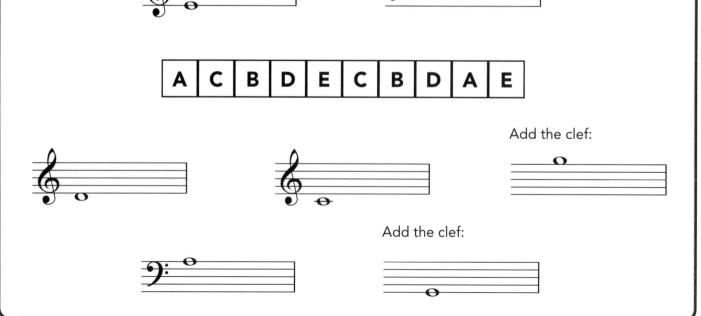

| A | C | B | D | E | C | B | D | A | E |

Add the clef:

Add the clef:

The grand stave

The right-hand 𝄞 and left-hand 𝄢 staves are joined together to make the **grand stave**, so you can play with both hands. Middle C sits in between the two staves.

20 Monster Middle C

Try all of these pieces as clapping or drumming duets with your teacher.

Can you sing these tunes?

21 In the court of King Henry

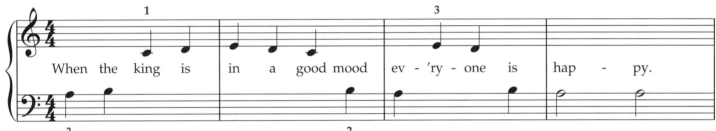

When the king is in a good mood ev - 'ry - one is hap - py.

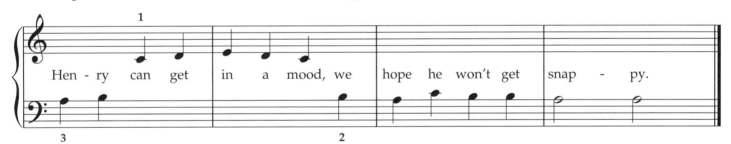

Hen - ry can get in a mood, we hope he won't get snap - py.

22 The tearful mouse

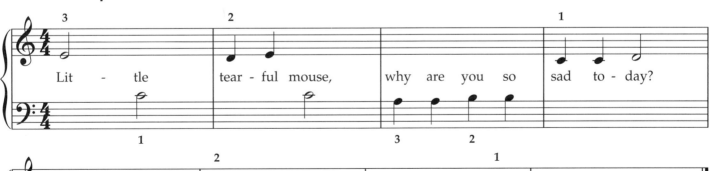

Lit - tle tear - ful mouse, why are you so sad to - day?

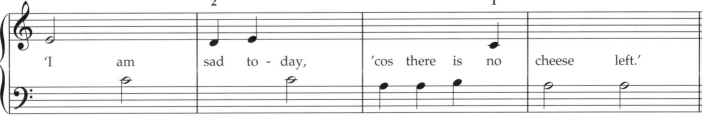

'I am sad to - day, 'cos there is no cheese left.'

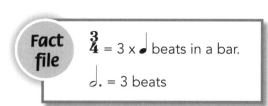

Fact file: $\frac{3}{4}$ = 3 x ♩ beats in a bar.

♩. = 3 beats

Clap the pulse of these tunes with the CD before you play them. Can you hear the three counts in each bar?

23 Dotty dance

Play - ing this song, don't get it wrong.

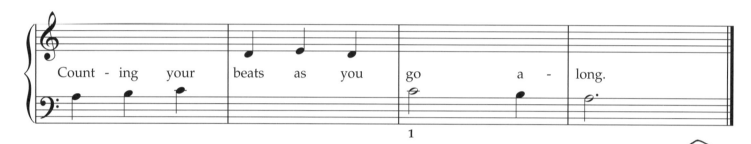

Count - ing your beats as you go a - long.

24 Dotty ditty

Sing the tunes as you play them.

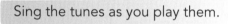

1 2 3 1 2 3 count - ing is fun!

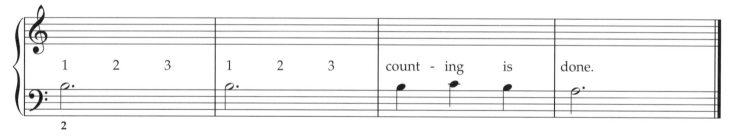

1 2 3 1 2 3 count - ing is done.

25 Dotty lotty ditty

Hey, ho, come to the fair.

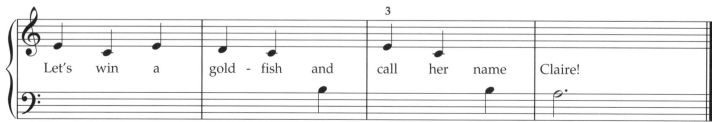

Let's win a gold - fish and call her name Claire!

Fact file

Signs which tell you how loudly or quietly to play are called **dynamics**. They are shown by their first letter in the music. Can you play the dynamics shown in these pieces?

f = **forte** = loud
mf = **mezzo forte** = moderately loud
mp = **mezzo piano** = moderately quiet
p = **piano** = quiet

26 I spy

27 Bulls-eye Bob

Listen to this on the CD first: can you hear where the loudest and softest parts are?

28 Chocolate-chip cookie

Sparkler

Let's get **sight-reading** … Have a look at this piece for a few moments then play it through. There is no CD track to help you – you have to work it out yourself!

Add the correct barlines to this tune:

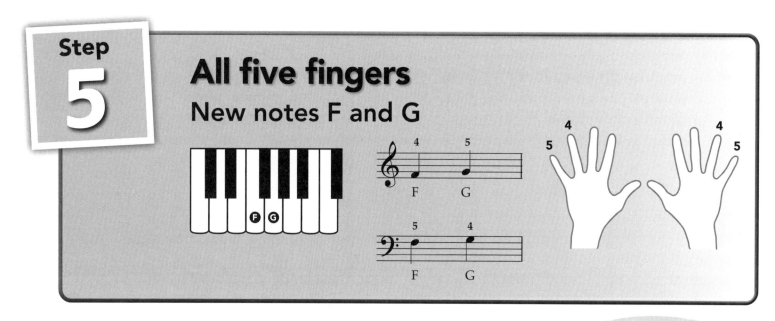

Step 5

All five fingers
New notes F and G

You are now ready to start using all five fingers of both hands.

Find all the Fs and Gs on the piano.

29 Right-hand study

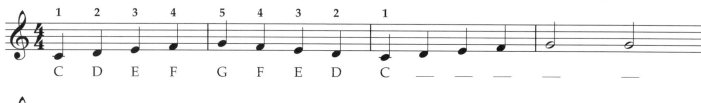

C D E F G F E D C — — — — —

I will prac - tise ev - 'ry day just like a bu - sy bee!

30 Left-hand study

Fill in the missing note names.

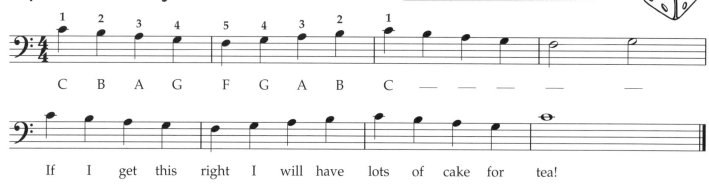

C B A G F G A B C — — — — —

If I get this right I will have lots of cake for tea!

Right-hand study accompaniment

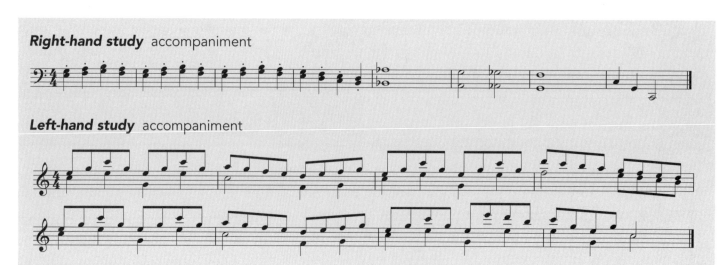

Left-hand study accompaniment

31 ## Creeping along

Try all these pieces as clapping duets. You clap one line, your teacher claps the other.

32 ## Popcorn

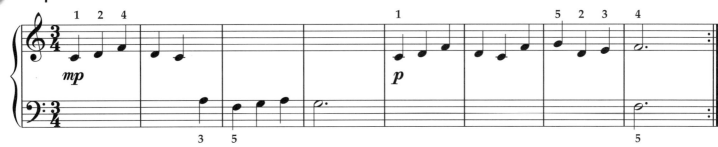

33 ## Pink fizz

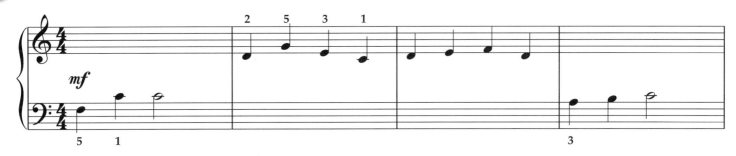

Can you remember what these dynamics mean?

mp means _____   *mf* means _____

f means _____   *p* means _____

A **metronome** produces regular clicks to help you keep 'in time' when you play along.

You can adjust the speed of the clicks – the number given is the number of clicks per minute (so ♩ – 60 means there will be 60 clicks each minute).

The Beats go on holiday

Fill in the note names to complete the story:

MRS MINIM _ I L L _ _ THE _ _ S _ S R _ _ _ Y

_ OR THE HOLIDAYS. THEY H _ _ NEVER _ _ _ N

TO _ M _ R I _ _ _ _ _ OR _ . ALL THE _ _ _ TS FAMILY

W _ R _ LOOKING _ ORW _ R _ TO VISITING _ LORI _ _ _ 'S

SP _ _ _ _ _ NTR _ . TH _ Y H _ D _ _ R _ _ _ T TIME

AND TRI _ _ ALL THE _ I _ _ _ R _ NT RIDES AND

INT _ R _ _ _ TIV _ _ _ _ M _ S.

Make up your own words using note-names:

Step 6

Introducing rests

Rests show a gap in the music, where the hands 'have a rest'.
Rests have the same names and lengths as notes:

𝄽 = **crotchet (quarter-note) rest** = 1 silent ♩ beat

𝄼 = **minim (half-note) rest** = 2 silent ♩ beats

𝄻 = **semibreve (whole-note) rest** = 4 silent ♩ beats,

or a whole bar's rest in any time signature

This is a **symphony** (a piece for orchestra) by Joseph Haydn. He wrote it especially to wake up a sleepy audience – they often nodded off at concerts after a big meal. The piece starts quietly but the sudden crash wakes them up!

When you come to a 𝄽 try blowing for one beat – this will help stop you playing when you should be resting!

34 The Surprise Symphony

Joseph Haydn

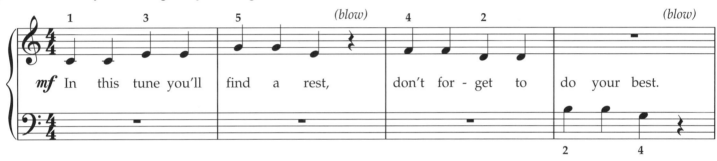

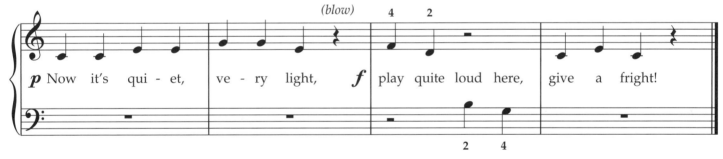

35 Resting beats

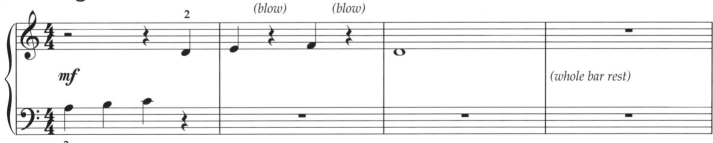

36 Penguins hop

37 Cuckoo clock blues

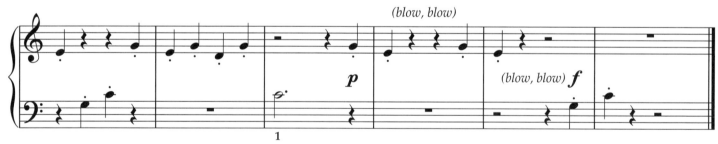

Penguins hop accompaniment

Fact file

Legato means to play smoothly, with no gaps between the notes. Legato notes are shown by a curved line called a **slur** joining them:

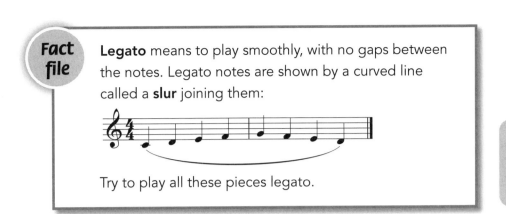

Try to play all these pieces legato.

Can you sing this piece? Singing to 'la' will help it sound legato.

Legato serenade 1

mf

Legato serenade 2

mf

Play this piece to your friends and family. Keep smiling as you perform!

(38) Snakes and adders

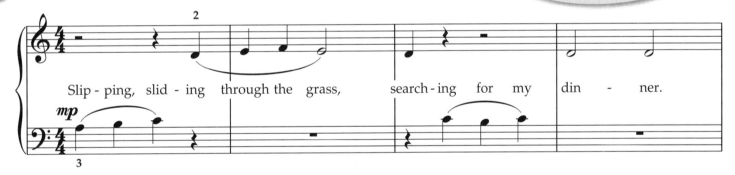

Slip - ping, slid - ing through the grass, search - ing for my din - ner.

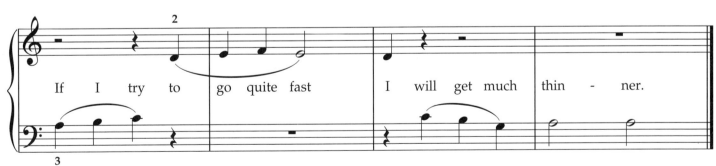

If I try to go quite fast I will get much thin - ner.

Snakes and adders accompaniment

mp

Tempo markings

You will often see a word (or words) at the top of a piece of music that describes how fast, and in what style, it should be played. Often it is in Italian, so you will need to learn what it means.

Allegro = quite quickly

Play 8va = play an octave (8 notes) higher than the notes are written

Playing duets is fun.
Ask your teacher for more!

The Cossacks are coming! Duet

39 This track is the teacher's part only; can you play along with it?

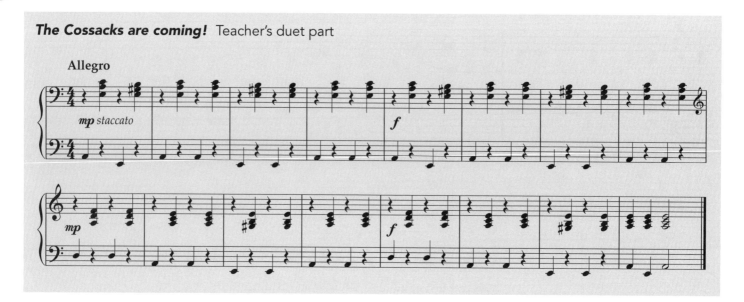

The Cossacks are coming! Teacher's duet part

Step 7

Introducing ♪ and ♫

Fact file

♪ ♪ = a **quaver** (or **eighth note**) = ½ count

When there is more than one quaver, they are joined together by a **beam**

♫ = 1 count   ♪ = a quaver (eighth-note) rest

Clap or drum these pieces before you play them.

My teacher

Traditional

My   tea-cher's got a   bun - ion, a   nose like a pick-led   o - nion, a

face   like   a squashed to - ma - to   and   legs   like   two   sticks!

40 Oranges and lemons

Traditional

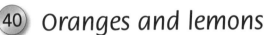

41 Scooby Doo, where are you?

Words and Music by Ben Raleigh and David Mook

Lively

mf

(blow)

f

(blow)

Low C

Once you've learnt these pieces, try **spotting changes** in them. Your teacher will play the rhythm of each to you, with one change each time. Can you hear what and where the change is?

42 Dance of the diplodocus

A bit ploddy!

43 Stegosaurus stomp

Make up your own dinosaur tune.

Heavy dance

44 Pterodactyl

Gliding

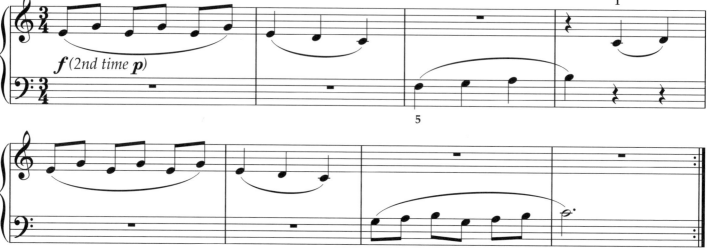

A musical crossword

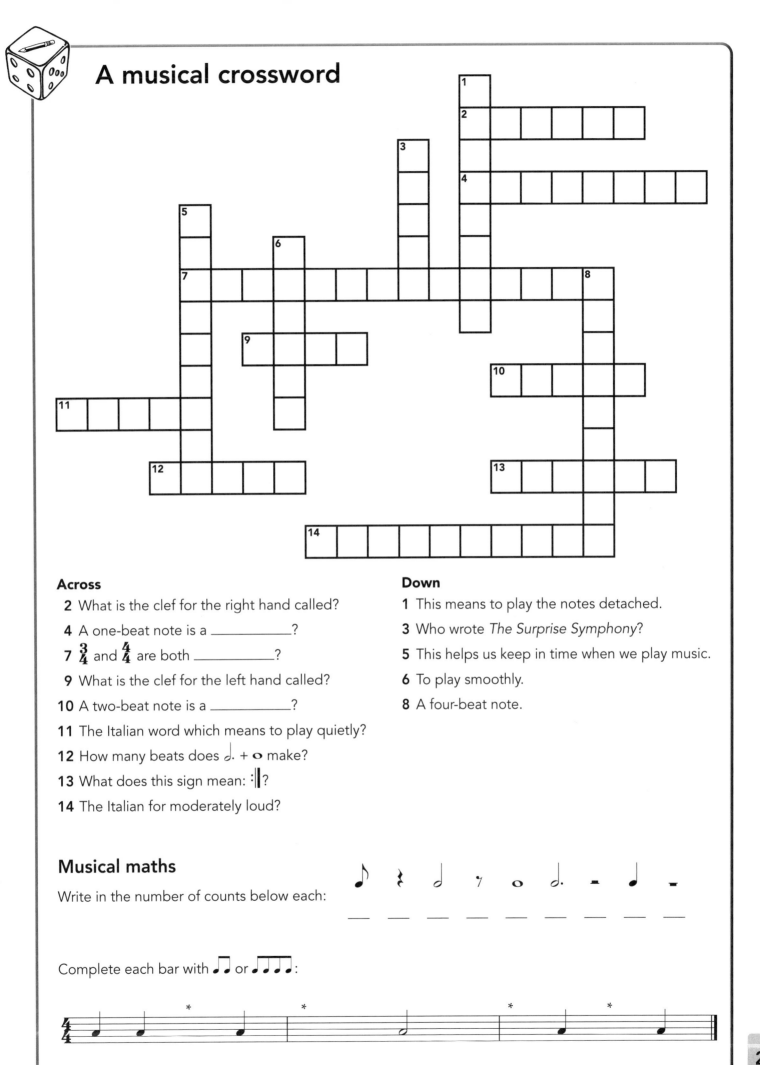

Across

2 What is the clef for the right hand called?

4 A one-beat note is a _____?

7 $\frac{3}{4}$ and $\frac{4}{4}$ are both _____?

9 What is the clef for the left hand called?

10 A two-beat note is a _____?

11 The Italian word which means to play quietly?

12 How many beats does ♩. + 𝅝 make?

13 What does this sign mean: 𝄇?

14 The Italian for moderately loud?

Down

1 This means to play the notes detached.

3 Who wrote *The Surprise Symphony*?

5 This helps us keep in time when we play music.

6 To play smoothly.

8 A four-beat note.

Musical maths

Write in the number of counts below each:

Complete each bar with ♫ or ♬:

Step 8

Hands together

You're now ready to start playing with both hands together. When you see notes above each other, you should play them at the same time.

Fact file

> = play the notes with an **accent**

Andante = at a walking pace

Moderato = at a moderate speed

Accel. (accelerando) = gradually getting faster

---

45 ## The angry wizard

---

46 ## The wheels on the bus are going flat!

Traditional

The wheels on the bus are going flat! accompaniment

47 Ode to joy

Listen to this track before you play it. Where is the softest part? Try singing the opening bars when you've listened to it.

Ludwig van Beethoven

Ludwig van Beethoven was born in 1770 in Germany. He was known for being short tempered and rather scruffy – he was once mistaken for a tramp and thrown in prison! Beethoven composed *Ode to joy* as the last movement of a choral symphony for orchestra and choir – he was deaf when he wrote it.

48 Express train

Listen to this piece, then describe the dynamics.

accel. (gradually getting faster)

Introducing B♭

Fact file

♭ is a **flat** sign. When you see a flat before a note it lowers it by one note – black or white. This is a B♭ on the keyboard:

Can you find all the B♭s on the piano? A flat sign before a note changes it for the whole bar.

Before you play these pieces, place your hands on the keys and make sure the second finger of your left hand is on the B♭ key.

(49) Footsteps in the night

With caution

(50) Good King Wenceslas

Traditional

(51) Lucky Jim

Always practise pieces hands separately first.

Allegro

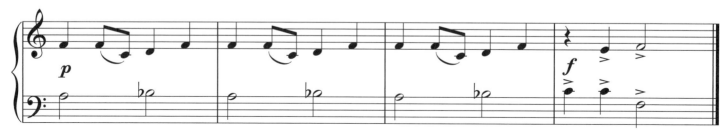

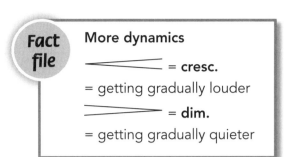

Fact file

More dynamics

= **cresc.**

= getting gradually louder

= **dim.**

= getting gradually quieter

52 Old MacDonald

Moderato

Traditional

53 *Rainy days*

Make up some words to fit the mood and rhythm of the music, then sing it.

Gentle showers

Put a ♮ before all the Bs in these bars and then play the piece:

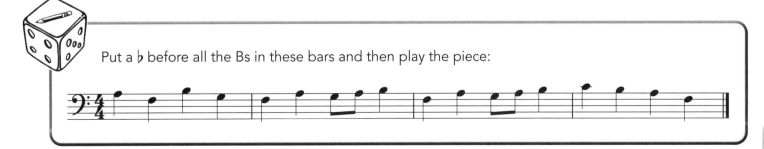

33

You may like to try *Sunny Side Up* from **Up-Grade! Piano Duets Grades 0–1** here.

Fact file **Two-note chords** When two notes or more are played together it is known as a **chord**. This piece starts on the 4th beat of the bar. This is called starting on an **upbeat**.

54 **The grand old Duke of York**

Listen to this track before you play it. Can you hear where the loudest and quietest parts are?

Traditional

In march time

55 **The green-eyed monster**

Listen to this track before you play it. Is it mainly legato or staccato?

Scary

(low F)

Sports

Can you make a rhythm to fit the names of the following sports?
The first few have been done for you …

Ice hockey	♩ ♫	Butterfly stroke	
Badminton	♫ ♩	Water polo	
Hundred metre dash	♪♪♪♪♪	Football	
Table tennis	♬♬	Marathon	
Swimming		Cross country ski-ing	

Football-boot challenge!

Connect each ball to the correct boot:

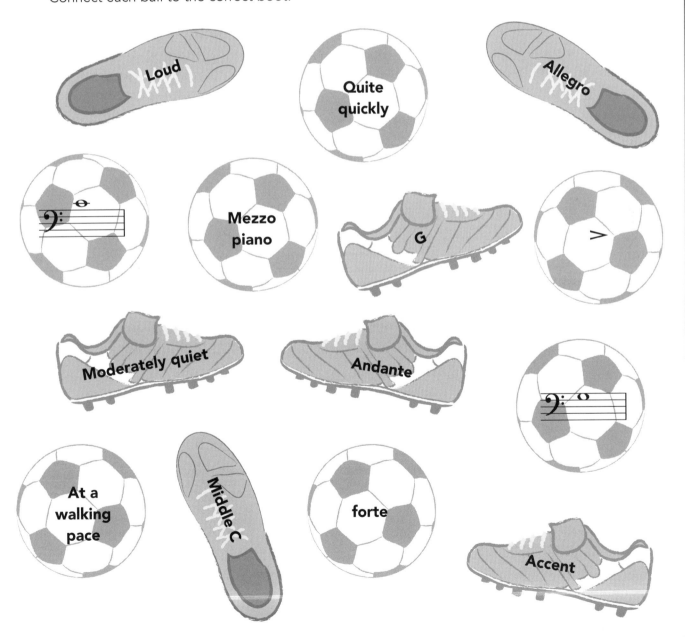

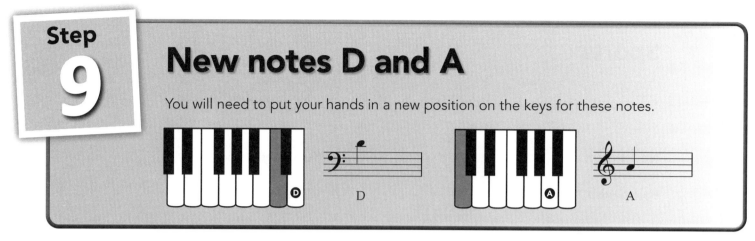

Step 9

New notes D and A

You will need to put your hands in a new position on the keys for these notes.

D   A

Onwards and upwards Duet

Fact file Poco = a little
Rit. = slower

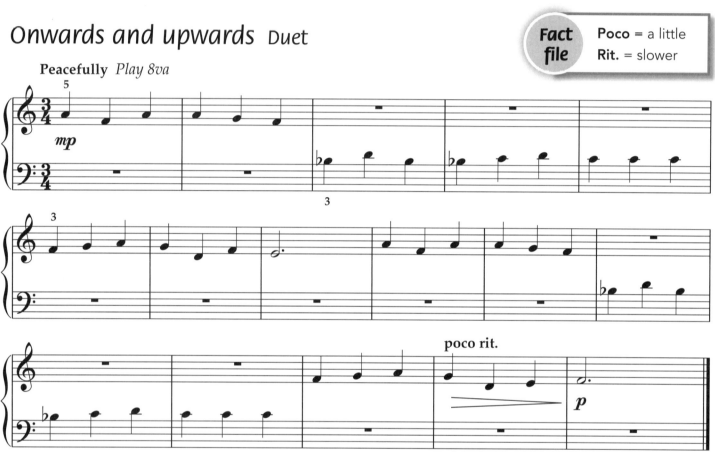

Peacefully *Play 8va*

poco rit.

56 This track is the teacher's part only; can you play along with it?

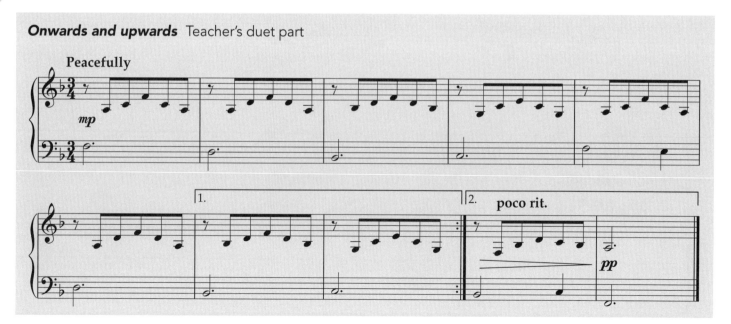

Onwards and upwards Teacher's duet part

Peacefully

Listen to this track before you play it or look through the music. Can you answer these questions?

- Did the music start loudly or softly? _____

- Was the left hand legato or staccato at the start? Did it change at all? _____

- Describe the mood of the music: _____

57 ## Catch me if you can?

Playfully

58 ## My bonnie lies over the ocean

You will need to extend your hand
to stretch six notes in this piece.

Smooth and calm

Traditional

Introducing F♯

Fact file

♯ is a **sharp** sign. When you see a ♯ before a note it raises it by one note – black or white.

This is an F♯:

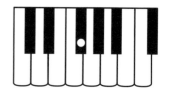

(59) ## Fiesta time

This is a great clapping or drumming duet – try it with your teacher!

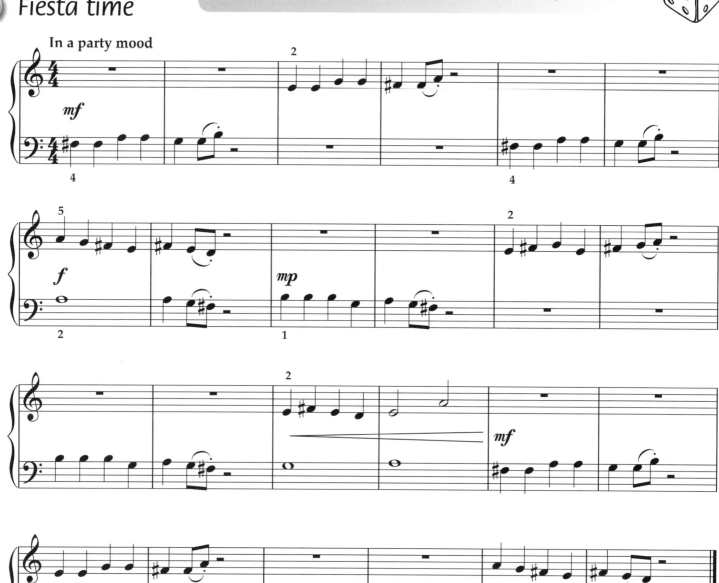

Put a ♯ before all the Fs and then play the piece:

Introducing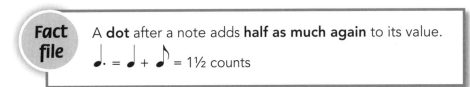

Fact file A **dot** after a note adds **half as much again** to its value.

♩. = ♩ + ♪ = 1½ counts

You can listen to the *New World Symphony* by **Antonín Dvořák** (pronounced D-Vor-shak) online. Dvořák was a famous Czech composer who lived from 1841–1904. He was a simple, mild-mannered man who had six children, kept pigeons and liked train-spotting!

Can you find all the C sharps on the keyboard?

Fact file **Largo** = slow and broad

60 Largo from the New World Symphony

Antonín Dvořák

61 Dotted boogie-on-down train!

Try to strengthen your weaker hand by using it to brush your teeth and your hair.

Higher and lower notes
Right-hand B and C

You will need to move your right hand to a new position to play these notes.

Making the right changes

Go-ing up the lad-der   till we get to A,   fur-ther up the lad-der, now you're on your way.

62 Supercalifragilisticexpialidocious

Words and Music by
Richard M. Sherman and Robert B. Sherman

A scale for the right hand

If you play all the right-hand notes you've learnt so far they make a **scale**.
You will need to tuck your thumb under to play the F so you don't run out of fingers!

(63) Hot potato

How many groups of four quavers can you spot? _____

How many Cs can you find in the right hand? _____

How many Bs can you find in the left hand? _____

Your teacher will play the first two bars with one change. Can you spot what it is?

You may like to try *Whirley Bird* from **Up-Grade! Piano Grades 0–1** here.

Left-hand C, D, E

You will need to move your left hand to a new position to play these notes.

C   D   E

Making the left changes

Can you name the notes on the way down?

Little bird

Traditional

1 3   2 4

 Fact file   ♩‿♩ = a **tie** joins two of the same note together.
Make sure you hold on through the second note of the tie.

64 Girls and boys

Can you sight-read the left-hand part on its own?

Clap the pulse of this piece with the CD. What is the time signature?

Traditional

Allegro

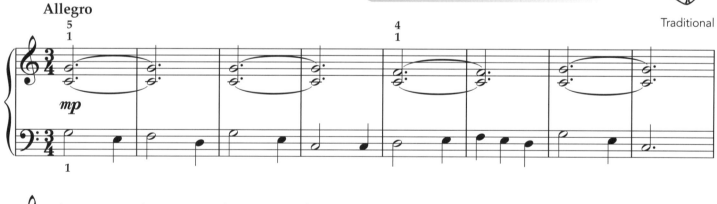

mp

f

You may like to try *Apple-Pie Waltz* from **Up-Grade! Piano Grades 0–1** here.

65 Country gardens

Your teacher will play the first line with one change. Can you spot what it is?

Traditional

66 Simple gifts

Can you sing this tune?

Traditional

A scale for the left hand

If you play all the left-hand notes you've learnt so far, they make a scale. You will need to bring your third finger over your thumb to play the A so that you don't run out of fingers!

43

Balloons

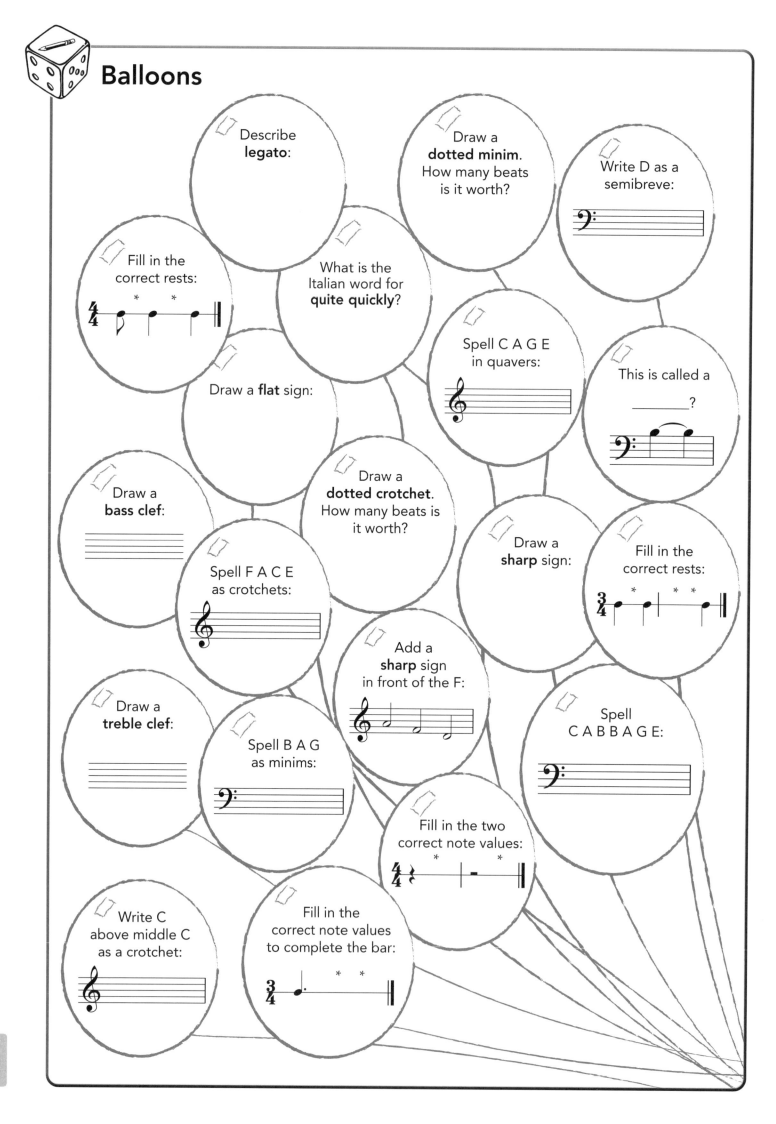

Recital pieces

Step **11**

Here are a selection of pieces for you to play for friends and family.
The CD tracks here are **backings** only so you can play the piano part on your own.

Fact file

pp = **pianissimo** = very quiet

ff = **fortissimo** = very loud

♪ = play this small note quickly before the main note – 'crush' them together!

67 **Lightning Ridge**

Draw a picture to describe this piece.

You may like to try *Give Me Joy* from **Up-Grade! Piano Duets Grades 0–1** here.

How many B flats can you spot in the piece? _____

Describe what happens when you see a **rit**. _____

Clap the pulse with the track.
What is its time signature?

Clapping duet: you clap one
line, your teacher claps the other.

68 Catch 22

With energy

69 Little Donkey

Fact file This piece has a **first and second time bar**. Play through to the first time
bar, then repeat the piece, jumping to the second time bar to finish.

Steady donkey speed!

Words and music by Eric Boswell

New note D

D

Fact file ⌢ = a **pause** means you hold the note for longer than its value

Listen to this piece before you learn it and describe the dynamics.

70 ## The rose

Words and music by Amanda McBroom

You may like to try *Make Way for the King* from **Up-Grade! Piano Grades 0–1**, and *Ping Pong* and *Dual Control* from **Really Easy Jazzin' About** with these pieces.

71 Be-bop

Be-bop is a style of jazz that is usually played quite fast.

How many B flats can you spot?

Clap the pulse whilst your teacher plays this piece.

Can you emphasize the first beat in each bar?

Try this as a clapping or drumming duet.

Can you compose your own be-bop piece with your teacher?

You've learnt to play your pieces,
You've learnt to count each bar.
You've learnt to play the 'Basics' way:
Well done, you are a STAR!

**Next stop:
Piano Basics
2!**